Stewards for the Earth

Earthrise

Carolyna Saint Germain

Clip Art from Microsoft Office Professional 2010 with permission from Microsoft; reference number 1232148057 (Deepak)

Balboa Press books may be ordered through booksellers or by contacting:

Balboa Press
A Division of Hay House
1663 Liberty Drive
Bloomington, IN 47403
www.balboapress.com
1 (877) 407-4847

ISBN: 978-1-4525-1512-0 (sc)
ISBN: 978-1-4525-1513-7 (e)

Library of Congress Control Number: 2014909222

Printed in the United States of America.

Balboa Press rev. date: 06/18/2014

BALBOA
PRESS
A DIVISION OF HAY HOUSE

Stewards for the Earth

One planet
One people
Allowing
Accepting
Appreciating

Earthrise

By
Carolyna Saint Germain

For all those who love the Earth

Acknowledgements

I wish to express my deepest gratitude and appreciation to the Mother Earth, for her sustenance, beauty, acceptance, allowance, inspiration and genuine kindness. Without Mother Earth as my muse, this book would not have been written.

I am also grateful for the technical expertise of my daughter Koa without whom I would still remain entangled in the "how do I do this" technical formatting confusion; to my son Beau for his immeasurable encouragement and patient editing; to my daughter Shayna who has taught me how to take risks because of her courageous example; and to all of my supportive family who believe in me, and honor their Mother.

Thank you to all of my spiritual teachers, fellow nature lovers and Earth-loving people who see the constant reflection of their humanity in Mother Earth, know it as a reality and live this truth.

Those who contemplate the beauty of the earth find reserves of strength that will endure as long as life lasts.

• • •

Those who contemplate the beauty of the earth find reserves of strength that will endure as long as life lasts.

• • •

There is symbolic as well as actual beauty in the migration of the birds, the ebb and flow of the tides, the folded bud ready for the spring.

There is something infinitely healing in the repeated refrains of nature - the assurance that dawn comes after night, and spring after the winter. -Rachel Carson-

Blessingways for the Earth

The Earth is our mother
We must take care of her (bis)
Hey yun yun Ho yun yun
Hey yun yun (bis) Native American

I have always loved the Great Outdoors: Mother Earth, Mother Nature, my planet, my home.

Growing up in Maine, I played outside from dawn until dark and long after dark too. I always feel best when outside, in the weather, with the wind, the sun, the rain and the snow. There are many of us that prefer to be in nature, no matter our age, our profession, our status. It is deeply enjoyable and most fulfilling.

The Earth is our prime mentor and source for god-like imitations. Through her unceasing and perpetual example, she demonstrates allowance and acceptance, of all things. Is that truly possible, and do we dare to be the same?

The oak grows next to the evergreen, the river runs into the sea, the wind and the rain are granted free rein. The Earth's natural possessions are resourced and consumed unrelentingly, without ever a grumble, nor an inkling of resentful bitterness. She is the ultimate, unsurpassed, unconditional Giver. In every aspect she exhibits compassionate coexistence and undeniable bounty. She displays exceptional qualities: unprecedented generosity, all-inclusive diversity, magnanimous acceptance and allowance, quiet wisdom and infinitely wide ranging magnificent beauty. She is clothed in vibrant colors, dramatic landscapes, and liquid light and shadow; offering all the possible hues, shades, textures, aromas, resonances, palettes, and perceptions. These are benevolent gifts, bestowed upon all of us who live here, without exception.

And she, this wonderful Mother Earth Planet, waits patiently for our acknowledgement and willful appreciation of her presence.

The Mother Earth, dramatically came to our attention as a global entity, and eradicated our old earth view and paradigm, in 1968 when Apollo 8 went to the moon. During the astronauts' preparations for this epic flight and experience, their total focus was on the moon and space. They were not thinking of what it would be like to look back on Earth. This vision of the Earth hanging in space, blue, white and green, rising above the moon's surface, left them utterly speechless. Their understanding, after they had this experience for the first time, was "that it (the experience of this view) was probably the most important reason we went". On Christmas Eve 1968, astronauts Frank Borman, James Lovell, and William Anders saw something no human had ever seen before—our planet, Mother Earth, as it appeared rising over the moon's horizon like a sunrise--their first Earthrise.

The photograph taken of that moment is one of the most iconic images of the 20th century. But interestingly enough, they almost missed taking it; the Earth disappears from their view just seconds after they successfully located the color film and snapped the shutter. Without that photo, the awe and power of that moment and the perspective it conveys, would never have been seen by the billions of humans whom it has touched in the years since. The impact of this vision is unsurpassable and allows us to understand the implications of how we interact with our Mother Planet Earth. This is why I chose it for the cover of *Stewards For The Earth.*

The astronauts were in awe. They experienced a total interconnection with the Earth. They saw her as a living breathing organism. This overview effect opened their minds and hearts to experience the Earth as not separate. It allowed for a cognitive shift to occur within each of them, initiating the idea that we are all one. This cognitive shift had a ripple effect, its impact reaching out to all of us that have seen this photo and beyond. The understanding carried such a great influence in our worldly culture that there were many of us that didn't need to see it to know and believe it. If the Earth dies, we will all die. It is time for us all to come up with a new story, a new paradigm, so that we can have a sustainable future. We've got to learn how to do this for ourselves because we are each responsible.

We all, individually and collectively, have this interconnection with the Earth, our home, our nurturing Mother. Because of space travel and scientific research, we are blessed with the gift of being able to "see" the planet hanging in space, with infinity behind it. We are given this vision without actually traveling to space. We get it.

It is vital, and significant, for us to be mindfully aware of Mother Earth, to observe her. It is important that we not allow her to wither away unseen. We have to take care of her as she takes care of us.

We *can* integrate our interconnection with the Earth within our daily lives. We can practice mindful awareness of her presence. By being in nature and outdoor places, there are powerful unconscious evocative reciprocal effects experienced between us and Mother Earth.

This mindful awareness and interconnection is our task, our mission, our joy and bliss as her Stewards.

And Mother Earth, responds to our connection, attention and appreciation.

Einstein revealed, and proved, that *everything* in the world, in the universe, *is energy*, and everything interacts even though we may not always have conscious awareness of it. All energy vibrates at particular frequencies. We humans are energy; each of us vibrating at a certain frequency. Our thoughts, feelings, beliefs and intentions determine the frequency of our energy. Given these variables, our energy shifts and changes, and can be focused and directed.

When we take a moment to make a conscious connection, we align our energy frequency to the energy frequency of our gaze, be it a flower, tree, cloud, glacier, mountain or sea. We share presence. We are mindfully aware. Mother Earth loves to be recognized in this way, and waits patiently for our noticing and viewing. And she in turn, notices us. We exchange appreciation energy. As we interact and bond with Mother Earth, she responds to us.

Mindful awareness, our conscious connection, is all it takes to be a *Steward for the Earth*. It doesn't take buying a hybrid automobile, or donating and demonstrating for ecological causes, although those commitments are certainly admirable and beneficial. One can simply take a conscious moment to notice, and love the Earth, the Nature, as you would a dear friend, a loved one, your Mother.

This book is about taking the moments to acknowledge and express your love, appreciation and caring for the Earth. With thoughtful conscious connection and mindful awareness, we create moments that I call *Blessingways*.

Blessingways

In peace and beauty may I walk… -csg-

• • •

The earth will
not continue
to offer its
harvest, except
with faithful
stewardship.
We cannot say
we love the
land and then
take steps to
destroy it for
use by future
generations.

• • •

Pope John Paul II~

Blessingways are meditative moments, filled with intention, prayer, and song. They are small personal ceremonies, rituals of behavior, acknowledgments of vision and being. A *Blessingway* is an experiential adventure into an unknown moment allowing for conscious connection.

Blessingways come from the diversity of our human experience, stories, myths and spiritualties. Like the diversity we see in nature, *Blessingways* are created from the diversity of our cultures, religions and spiritual practices. They are completely non-sectarian and not dogmatic; but rather practical, "down-to-earth" and of a daily nature. *Blessingways* have no restrictions on how, where or when, and they can be performed alone or with a group.

The experience of a *Blessingway* leaves a lasting impression, and strongly influences you to reinforce or change your assumptions, attitudes or expectations. It is both intellectually and emotionally satisfying. The energy frequency of your thought goes forth and creates a spiraling circle of energy frequencies. It is like the ripples formed from a dropped stone in still water. This pulsing energy reverberates through nature as it ripples out into the Earth, and returns to you, offering acceptance, allowance and appreciation for your intentions and attention. It resonates with the beating of your heart.

Blessingways are our conscious gifts to Mother Earth.

As our archetype and superstar of daily and steadfast gift giving, she receives our gifts and responds to our energy frequencies, authentically welcoming and appreciative of our sincere intentions.

Blessingways allow us that moment to hold conscious attention and be mindfully aware of our environment. We can listen to the voices of the grasses and become aware of the scents of the flowers, we can learn from the trees, and actually think like a plant. We can read the old myths on the rocks, in the caves, and in the deep of the forest's shade. We can hear the songs in the rippling mountain streams, in the rustling of the leaves, the soughing of the trees and see the spirit energy in the storm clouds and in the evening mists.

It doesn't matter who you are, or what your belief is. We, the Earth's people, are all different, and differences are like the myriad flowers in a meadow, the varied trees in a wood, the inimitable singularity of waves incessantly rolling unto the beach. Like these fine natural displays, our sameness articulates itself in the fact that we all share the same Earth. Our presence here remains the prime demonstration and manifestation that we are All One on the Mother Earth.

Song and Poetry

When we are deeply moved by natural beauty or great compassion, and ordinary speech no longer suffices to express this movement of energy and emotion, songs and poetry can fill the gap, allowing expression, the heart and soul's expression.

Song represents a profound relationship between the energy frequency of spirit and that of the mind. Song is the energy frequency of our breath, emerging from within our human organism, giving voice to our spirit, our soul, our heart. It can be likened to the illumined soul shining through human eyes for it is the brilliance of one's spirit vocalizing the inexpressible, with a heartfelt and moving song.

Songs are thoughts, intuitive inspirations sung with the breath, our spirit breath of life. It is a natural way to be intimate with and aware of, the plants, trees, flowers, and all of nature. Songs are part of a frequency encyclopedia on the sonic level, in the same way that seeds represent plants and flowers on their physical level.

The Earth is bursting with wordless sounds and songs. Indigenous people, and all people that live, or spend long days in nature, are acutely aware and conscious of the natural world's sounds and frequencies. They know how to listen for the mysterious power permeating all of nature which allows Mother Earth to speak and to sing. She expresses herself in harmonics: songs without words. We can also sing without words, because it is the sound and harmonics that allow spirit a conduit of expression. Poetic expression may sometimes follow the harmonics.

When I express prayer and intentions through song, Mother Earth, seems to listen in, and all things around me seem to come to attention and be present. We come together. The environment and I become one and it feels like interspecies communication is possible. The songs of the plants, the rocks, the waters, the sky and the Mother Earth herself infuse my life more and more. All of life has song and it carries me along in its patterns of frequency. It opens my heart and I am blessed by the circular sharing of these harmonics, chants and poetic words. *Blessingways* help us to connect and be a part of Mother Earth, and songs allow us to intimately and artistically express our relationship.

A small compilation of songs that have graced my life over the last fifty years is offered. May it serve as an example of what you can do when you allow yourself the experience, accepting the simple beauty and privilege of the inspiration that is presented by nature and comes forth from within.

I encourage you to sing your own songs. Song is a splendid part of a *Blessingway.*

The duet between Mother Earth and a human being is a love song. ~csg~

Blessingways

Each of these *Blessingways* is but an offering of the unlimited possibilities that you can create and experience.

A Steward for the Earth practices moments of mindful awareness and has conscious connection to the Earth: Mother Earth~Mother Nature.

This attentiveness is always a *Blessingway*, no matter the duration. Time only matters to those of us who have clocks. A second is infinitely vast on the frequency level.

I see you in the stars,
    the blades of grass,

        the grains of sand.

Many of us,
    honoring,

        loving the Mother. -csg-

And so, With a Boundless Heart,
Should One Cherish ALL Living Things

-Buddah-

While you are appreciating and loving the Earth, you are appreciating and loving yourself. -csg-

The moment one gives close attention to anything, even a blade of grass, it
becomes a mysterious, awesome, indescribably magnificent world in itself.

-Henry Miller-

Blessingways

for You,

to Experience at Your Leisure…

The Spirit of the plants
has come to me

in the form of a beautiful dancing green woman

(bis)

And her eyes fill me with peace,
her dance fills me with peace (bis)

~Lisa Theil

Notes and Reflections

Acknowledge a Tree

What do you see?

How does it grow, does it follow the sun, is the bark smooth, rough, layered, does it peel, what is the foliage like, are the leaves big, small, do they change color, are they pointed, are they needles, can you see the roots, can you see the sky through the branches?

Is it talking to you? Can you hear its song?

Do you feel its embrace? Can you give it a hug?

I frequently tramped eight or ten miles through the deepest snow to keep an appointment with a beech-tree, or a yellow birch, or an old acquaintance among the pines. ~ Henry David Thoreau~

15

Notes and Reflections

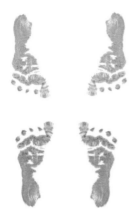

Barefoot on the Earth

In the grass, in the sand, on the rocks, in the water, creek, pond, lake, ocean, in the leaves, pine needles, in the dirt, in the garden, in the mud, on the gravel, on the pavement, on the cement,

How does it feel? Is it coarse, smooth, sharp, soft, angular, is it wet, dry, squishy, what's the temperature, cool, warm, cold, hot, does it make you want to make a sound with your breath? OOOO AAAA EEEE UUUU

Forget not that the earth delights to feel your bare feet, and the wind longs to play with your hair. -Kahlil Gibran-

Notes and Reflections

Watch the Clouds

Lay in the grass, on the sand, on the water, watch the sky fill, and empty, and fill again, with clouds.

Constant motion, it's like being able to see the wind.

Such a huge diversity of size, shapes, colors, depth, light and shadow,

The cloud people are talking to you.

Listen.

You must not blame me if I do talk to the clouds. ~Henry David Thoreau~

Notes and Reflections

 # Stick in the Water

Throw a stick into a creek, river, eddy, bay, ocean.

Watch where it goes, willingly, freely, with the flow, banged around a bit in the current, floating, bobbing, twirling, twisting, allowing the movement to carry it, surrendering to the energy of the flow.

Throw the stick while on a bridge and see it come out the darkness of the other side, unscathed, merrily, merrily, merrily, merrily, the stick is in a dream. It is singing with the brook.

Hear it. Allow yourself to BE it.

Come forth into the light of things.
Let nature be your teacher. ~ William Wordsworth~

Notes and Reflections

Sunrise

Get up for Sunrise. Go outside, light a fire, an incense stick, a pipe, a candle, a flame, a burning ember to greet the fire of the Sun.

Speak your intentions and prayers out loud to Father Sun, Mother Earth and Sacred Fire. Have a spirit of gratitude for your Life and the Life of all your Relations: human, animal, plant and mineral, the elements, fire, air, earth and water. Welcome the awakening of a new day with an open heart and child-like innocence.

Welcome Song ~Native American~
(repeat four times acknowledging the four directions: North, South, East and West)
Hey ai ai ai ai un gu wah (x7)
Un gu wah Un gu wah

Notes and Reflections

Moonglow

Have you ever really noticed the moon…from the mysterious Cheshire cat smile to the full face of illuminated night time glory, and emptying into the absence of light. It only takes 28 days to see this jam-packed cycle, and it repeats over and over again, influencing, and even controlling, the oceans tides, the growth of plants, and the growth of the hair on your head.

Choose a month or two, go outside into the night and observe the cycle. Some call her the Grandmother, others say it is the Man in the moon. Your choice.

Howl and sing!

Hey ya hey ya hey ya hey ya hey ya hey heyya…henne ho! (x4)

~Native American~Full Moon Song

Notes and Reflections

Spring

The great awakening! The resurrection. The renaissance. The renewal. The first season in the annual quarterly rotation of the Mother planet Earth. It happens of its' own accord and there is no stopping spring.

Become a part of it by planting something: a seed, a bulb, a flower, an herb, a vegetable, a bush, a shrub, a tree. Tell the seedling what your intentions are in the planting and make a commitment to care, feed, and observe it bloom and grow.

Life unceasing, unfolding, blossoming, where it is planted.

Think about it. You are a part of that. Spring shows us how the Earth awakens from the dream.

Never yet was a springtime, when the buds forgot to bloom.
—Margaret Elizabeth Sangster

Notes and Reflections

Looking Glass

What I am looking at, I am. It is all a mirror.

Go choose a spot to sit, in the park, by the water, on the beach, in the forest, in your back yard, on your balcony, anywhere.

Observe the environment. "See" what is around you. Know that you are within all that you see, and what you see is within you. Microcosm and macrocosm, you are the mirror of it all. Allow this moment.

Forests, lakes, and rivers, clouds and winds, stars and flowers, stupendous glaciers and crystal snowflakes - every form of animate or inanimate existence leaves its impress upon the soul of man. ~Orison Swett Marden~

Notes and Reflections

Rain

"It's raining, it's pouring, the old man is snoring, went to bed and he bumped his head and he couldn't get up in the morning. Rain, rain, go away, come again some other day."

~Old English Nursery Rhyme~

That's how most of us feel about rain…but what if we didn't? What if just once you went out into the rain and got soaked, or bundled up and stayed dry except your face, or went into a pond, or pool, or the sea and lowered your eyes to the level of the water and watched the rain drops land and merge into the vast oneness of the water you are submerged in. Try it. One time.

Rain: a most precious gift.

Can't live without it.

Let the rain kiss you. ~Langston Hughes~

Notes and Reflections

Art

Mother Nature is a magnificent Artist. She uses flowers, plants, shrubs and trees; and clouds, sunrises, sunsets, and stars, as paint; and the earth and sky as the empty canvas. What marvelous art!

Create your own personal work of art using horticulture, on your land, in your yard, flowerbox, or pot. Choose your palette of colors, shapes and sizes. Allow your creative spirit to come forth. See your expression emerge as your "canvas" blossoms and unfolds.

A new experience maybe…just try it. The natural artist in you is waiting. Express yourself.

Everybody needs beauty as well as bread…. -John Muir-

Notes and Reflections

Birds

Look in the sky and the trees for the birds, as you walk, drive, sit outside or stare out your window. What species are they? What are they are doing: flying, soaring, sitting still, pecking, jawing, cooing, cawing, shrieking, singing.

What does their characterization represent, or mirror, in your personal expression and experience?

What occurs in your life after you've acknowledged them? Appreciate and accept the "message", the insight, and guidance. What does the simple watching of them bring to you.

Observing them you are observing yourself.

A bird does not sing because it has an answer, it sings because it has a song.
~chinese proverb~

Notes and Reflections

Rocks and Stones

Find a stone. Notice the shape, size and colors. Carry it around for a few days in your pocket. It is a noticeable piece of Mother Earth that you can hold close to your heart, in your hand, maybe small and clean enough to put in your mouth.

Spin a little spell of heartfelt words and breathe it on the stone. Then, let it go. Throw it as far as you can, or skip it across the water; drop it from your balcony, or just lay it in the grass. Walk away. You have left a part of yourself with the Earth, forever.

Rocks pray too.
Pebbles and boulders and old weathered hills.
They are still and silent, and those are two
important ways to pray. -Douglas Wood-

Notes and Reflections

Flowers

There are many varieties of flowers, even more diverse than our global human community; and they express our heart's truest language.

Visit a flower shop, or look around at your local market. Which variety would you give to your friend, your mother, your lover, your neighbor, your teacher, your grandmother? Why that one? What does it silently convey that you would want to verbally say. Give one away.

You can plant a row, or a pot of flowers, just for giving away. Flowers leave some of their fragrance on the hand that bestows them.

They are the language of your heart.

Earth laughs in flowers. ~Ralph Waldo Emerson~

Notes and Reflections

Elements

The Earth, the Fire
    the Water, The Air

Return, Return,
    Return Return (Bis)

Hey a hey a hey a hey a
Ho a ho a ho a ho (Bis)
~Celtic Chant~

Notes and Reflections

Air

"Sometimes…all I need is the air that I breathe…" ~1974 the Hollies~

Something we take for granted and never think about: Air

Take a few moments to breathe in the air at different times of the day: pre-dawn, sunrise, mid-day, late afternoon, dusk, early evening, nighttime, after midnight. How is it different?

And during different weather: in the crisp cold, on a snowy day, on a rainy day, in the warm sunshine, just before a thunder storm, when it is completely still, when it's blustery and blowing. What is different?

Breathe. Acknowledge the life force that is

AIR.

Notes and Reflections

Fire

Fire is magic, mystery, destruction, and creation. If the Mother Earth has no fire, she would perish and yet fire also destroys her.

Light a night fire and watch the sparks spiral up to the sky carrying your thoughts, prayers, intentions skyward. Lose yourself in the flames.

Contemplate this action of burning flames, molten lava, dissolving, consuming, leaving behind new earth, new growth.

Appreciate and respect the cycle/spiral/circle.

Without Fire, we would perish, and Fire perishes all.

It is a fire that consumes me, but I am the fire.
~Jorge Luis Borges~

Notes and Reflections

Water

Water ~ the Life-bearer. All life begins in water. Our brain is 80% water.

Without water everything metamorphoses and living forests, plants, animals and humans die.

Drink a glass of water noticing how each swallow slips down your throat effortlessly and beneficially.

Pour water unto the earth and notice that it too receives the water graciously and appreciatively.

Notice and appreciate the waters of Life in their many forms: wells, springs, creeks, rivers, ponds, lakes, oceans and from your faucet.

Water is the BEST of all things. ~Pindar, 438 B.C. Olympian Odes ~

Notes and Reflections

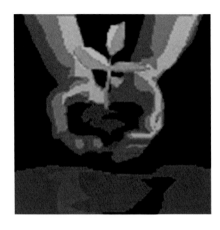

Earth

All sustenance is derived from earth: dirt and soil, the ground,

Hold some dirt in your hands. Feel it. Smell it. Thank it for growing your food, keeping you healthy and alive. Love it.

In your imagination, see the frequency of that love spreading throughout the dirt of the whole globe: rich brown dirt, loam, moss, gravel, clay, silt, desert sand, and white and black beach sand.

Then…let the soil from your hand return to the dirt family on the ground. Nourished by your love.

A nation that destroys its soils destroys itself. ~Franklin D. Roosevelt ~

Notes and Reflections

"The love of dirt is among the earliest of passions,
as it is the latest.
Mud-pies gratify one of our first and best instincts.
So long as we are dirty, we are pure.

Fondness for the ground comes back to a man
after he has run the round of pleasure and
business, eaten dirt, and sown wild oats, drifted
about the world, and taken the wind of all its
moods.
The love of digging in the ground (or of looking
on while he pays another to dig) is as sure to come
back to him, as he is sure, at last, to go under the
ground, and stay there."

~Charles Dudley Warner~

Notes and Reflections

Summer

Summer feels good. The warm sun on our less-clothed skin, the long, lazy days and short balmy nights, the blooming of flowers and plants, vegetables growing, grain fields reaching for the sky, trees sprouting fruits and nuts. Easy to love…

How is that plant doing that you planted in the spring? Is its face turning towards the sun, stretching towards the sky? Is your face turning towards the sun? Accept and experience the warm grace of Summer.

Summer is the time when one sheds one's tensions with one's clothes, and the day is jeweled balm for the battered spirit. A few of those days and you can become drunk with the belief that all's right with the world. -Ada Louise Huxtable-

Notes and Reflections

Window Open

Have you slept with your window open? Have you allowed the night air to caress your face, infiltrate your dreams?

Open your window and smell the night air. What is different about the night air from the daytime? Can you see the moon and the stars from your bed?

Breathe in the mystery the night air contains. Ask the spirit of the night to fill your dreams with your deepest secret wish.

The stars are forth, the moon above the top of the snow shining mountains... Beautiful! I linger yet with Nature, for the night hath been to me a familiar face; and in her starry shade of dim and solitary loveliness I learn'd the language of another world. -Lord Byron-

Notes and Reflections

Sunset

Watch the sun disappear on your horizon at sunset; it doesn't matter what your horizon looks like, it's that point where the earth meets the sky in your view as you face west. Let the sun take you along as it slowly sinks into the infinite beyond of what you see as the line's edge, dropping ever so slowly… into someone's sunrise.

Dusk is just an illusion because the sun is either above the horizon or below it. And that means that day and night are linked in a way that few things are. There cannot be one without the other, yet they cannot exist at the same time. How would it feel to remember to be always together yet forever apart?

Sunsets are quite old fashioned. To admire them is a distinct sign of provincialism of temperament. Upon the other hand, they go on. ~Oscar Wilde~

Notes and Reflections

Trees

The tree which moves some to tears of joy is, in the eyes of others, only a green thing that stands in the way. Some see nature all ridicule and deformity ... and some scarce see nature at all. But to the eyes of the man of imagination, nature is imagination itself. -William Blake ~

Today I have grown taller from walking with the trees. ~Karle Wilson Baker~

Few are altogether deaf to the preaching of pine trees. Their sermons on the mountains go to our hearts; and if people could be got into the woods, even for once, to hear the trees speak for themselves, all difficulties in the way of forest preservation would vanish. -John Muir~

Notes and Reflections

Choose one tree and befriend it.

Watch it begin to bud in the early spring and onward to summer, unfolding to its fullness; then to altering autumn and the deep dream-sleep of winter.

What changes does it go through, what storms does it survive, what nurtures it to reach fullness; does it have a flower, do the seeds blow in the wind, does the bark change color, do the leaves turn inside-out before the rains come.

Is it ever-green, and what does that really mean, or do the leaves turn amazing and dazzling colors from baby spring green, to high summer brilliant green, to bright golden orange, only to float away on a windy autumn day, allowing the tree to be freely naked in the world. Only to deep sleep again, and dream a new dream.

You ever notice that trees do everything to get attention we do, except walk?
-Alice Walker, *The Color Purple, 1982*

Notes and Reflections

Forest Bathing

The Japanese engage in "Shinrin-yoku" which literally means "forest bathing," but it doesn't involve soaking in a tub among the trees. It refers to spending time in the woods for its therapeutic effect.

You can feel tension slip away in the midst of trees and nature's beauty. Science confirms forests' healing influence on the body. When you spend a few hours on a woodland hike, you breathe in phytoncides. These are the active substances released by plants and trees to protect them against insects and from rotting, which lowers blood pressure and stress and boosts your immune system.

Go to the woods, or to the park, or a tree-lined avenue and breathe the air, and bathe. It's the wonder of Mother Nature-Mother Earth. Try it.

In every walk with nature one receives far more than he seeks. ~John Muir~

Notes and Reflections

It is not so much for its beauty that the forest makes a claim upon men's hearts, as for that subtle something, that quality of air that emanation from old trees, that so wonderfully changes and renews a weary spirit. ~Robert Louis Stevenson~

The clearest way into the Universe is through a forest wilderness. ~ John Muir ~

Trees outstrip most people in the extent and depth of their work for the public good. ~Sara Ebenreck~ American Forests

Notes and Reflections

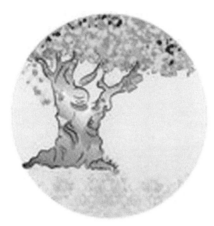

Autumn

It is almost like Mother Nature has saved up for this grand finale. The air is crisp, the days are shorter, and the leaves are turning a riot of colors.

Choose a tree and watch the leaves change each day. Choose a leaf and observe the transforming colors. Can you be there when it lets go, swirling and falling in the brisk wind of Fall. Can you lie under a tree that "rains leaves" and be buried under their beauty and scent. What is that like?

Press a leaf in a book and let it dry, a remembrance of autumn on your holiday tree.

Autumn is a second Spring when every leaf is a flower. ~Albert Camus~

Notes and Reflections

Wish on the Moon

When the Moon is new and barely a crescent, you can hang things on it, like a bucket. In the bucket you can put a wish, a dream, an intention, a prayer.

As you watch the moon become fuller each night, you will see that your bucket is becoming filled with the light of the moon.

Until…finally…when the moon is full, the bucket disappears and your wish has become part of the great starry sky, twinkling and shining into manifestation. Just a story? Maybe, but then again, maybe not. Try it.

When you wish upon a star
Makes no difference who you are
Your dreams come true.

~Cliff Edwards for Pinocchio~

Notes and Reflections

Sadness and Sorrow

Sometimes we are sad, and sorrow fills our hearts. We don't know where to go or what to do.

Go outside. Find a space where you can dig a hole. It doesn't have to be a big hole; the size of a cup will do.

Now this is the hardest part: think and remember why you are sad and heart broken. Pay attention to the details. Take all these images and put them in the hole in the ground. Take as long as you like and put in a much as you have. Mother Earth can hold them all.

When you feel that everything is in the hole, bury them. Mother Earth will hold them in safekeeping should you want them again. But otherwise know that these feelings are no longer a part of you. You've let them go.

Every man has his secret sorrows which the world knows not.
~Henry Wadsworth Longfellow~

Notes and Reflections

Winter

All is still, bright, clean and white after a snow. The air is cold, crisp and your nostrils stick together when you first go outside and breathe in the sharpness.

Frost grows on the window panes, forming lovely whorl patterns. Breathe on the glass. You give frost more ammunition; it can build castles and cities and whole ice continents with your breath. Listen. Hear the crackle of the snow fairies' wings.

Have you noticed when it snows, it is so still and quiet. Be as still and quiet as new falling snow in the black of night. Does the snow love the trees and fields as it quietly covers them up snug with soft white quilts? Can you snuggle down into your bed and love yourself the same way. And dream the dream of a new dream.

Nature looks dead in winter because her life has gathered into her heart.
~ Hugh MacMillan~

Notes and Reflections

*When we contemplate the whole globe as one great dewdrop,
striped and dotted with continents and islands, flying through
space with other stars, all singing, and shining together as one,
the whole universe appears as an infinite storm
of beauty* -John Muir-

Notes and Reflections

The earth is our mother. Whatever befalls the earth befalls the sons and daughters of the earth. This we know. All things are connected like the blood which unites one family. All things are connected.
Whatever befalls the earth befalls the sons and daughters of the earth. We did not weave the web of life, we are merely strands in it. Whatever we do to the web we do to ourselves. ~Chief Seattle~

Songs Recorded by St.Robert Recording Studios, Olympia WA

www.stewardsfortheearth.com to listen and download songs offered.

The duet between Mother Earth and a human being is a love song.

Sing your song.

As long as I live, I'll hear waterfalls and birds and winds sing.
I'll interpret the rocks, learn the language of flood, storm, and the avalanche.
I'll acquaint myself with the glaciers and wild gardens, and get as near the
heart of the world as I can. -John Muir-

Printed in the United States
By Bookmasters